TOPO

The Stories
Behind the Maps

By Jim West

TOPO

The Stories
Behind the Maps

By Jim West

Bristlecone Publishing
Lakewood, Colorado

Contents

Visit Us Online
119

Acknowledgements

I owe my time at the USGS map store to Rob Gray who hired me five months after he became manager. Thank you, Rob, for your confidence in me and for the gem you made of the map store. It is because of you this book came to be.

I am grateful to my co-worker and friend Rusty Dersch for his contributions to the stories contained in this book. Rusty and I worked together at the map store for more than five years and several stories in this book are his.

Special thanks are also due Roland Holtz for the entertaining stories he provided from his experiences as manager of the Mapsco map store in Denver and later as manager of the USGS map store. Roland's stories from his time at Mapsco are delightful.

Thank you to my editors, Leslie Miller for making the book "un-put-downable," and Chandra Wheeler for proofreading and copy editing.

Veronica Yager at YellowStudios created the book design and website and moved the book from manuscript stage to finished product. Thank you,

Veronica, for your professionalism and all your work.

This book would not be a reality without the help and inspiration of my loving wife, Ann. Her help in editing and her publishing ideas helped bring this book to life. For 32 years she has owned her own marketing business. In 2012 she launched Bristlecone Publishing to publish an award-winning lift-the-flap children's board book written and illustrated by our granddaughter when she was 12. This book is her second publication.

Finally, I would like to thank all the hikers, climbers, hunters, geologists, and map lovers who visited the map store and shared their stories with me. It is to them I owe this book.

Introduction

Why do people buy topographic maps?

I worked at the map store at the United States Geological Survey (USGS) in Denver for nine years. During that time I found that most people who buy maps fall into one of three groups: hikers, hunters, and geologists.

But I also learned that the reasons some people buy maps are more unusual and varied than I ever imagined. These people don't fit into categories.

Their stories are sometimes personal and poignant and sometimes hilarious. My most memorable are included in this book.

All the stories are true as told to me and my colleagues by actual map store customers. I have recalled the dialogue and details of each story to the best of my memory.

In 1879, Congress and the president consolidated the various geologic and geographical surveys underway at the time under the umbrella of a new federal agency, the USGS. Its task was to map the U.S. and then provide those maps to interested parties. Subsequently the USGS opened retail outlets in Reston, Virginia, Menlo Park, California, and Denver, Colorado.

The sale of USGS maps began to decline with the advent of new technology and increased competition from other map makers such as National Geographic and Latitude 40. To enhance sales, the USGS signed a contract with the Rocky Mountain Conservancy (RMC) (formerly Rocky Mountain Nature Association) in March, 2004, to sell maps for the agency and manage its map store.

I began work in the Denver map store in August 2004.

RMC is a non-profit organization head-quartered in Estes Park, Colorado.

Founded in 1931, the RMC assists over 50 different public land areas through the sale of interpretive materials at its many retail operations. Its flagship store is in the visitor center at Rocky Mountain National Park. The RMC produces educational publications, offers seminars, and supports research. It also provides aid and philanthropic support to Rocky Mountain National Park and its other public lands partners.

Initially the only products sold at the map store were USGS maps. But under Rob Gray's creative management, the store rapidly expanded. Within a few years, it was not only selling maps but hundreds of book titles and a vast array of other interesting merchandise. These included animal hand puppets, games, stuffed animals, globes, historic maps, and a wide selection of Trails Illustrated maps.

Word spread quickly and our sales and customer base grew steadily. When the weather warmed in the spring, geologists would flock to the store to get maps for the areas in which they were working. In the fall, hunters would congregate in the store looking for maps that showed private and public land so they could plan their hunts accordingly. And sales were buoyed by the popularity of our many other outdoor-related items.

But despite RMC's best efforts, the sale of USGS maps continued their steady decline in the wake of the 2008 recession and the increased use of electronic devices in lieu of paper maps.

The USGS map store closed in July 2013 when RMC, citing diminishing revenues, decided not to renew its contract with the USGS. Today the USGS sells maps only online and by mail.

We were not surprised that the store closed, but we were all saddened. I have had numerous friends and acquaintances tell me how disappointed they were in the loss of the store.

Although the USGS map store is gone, my memories are not. I wrote this book as a living testimony to all the people who visited the map store, to their memorable stories behind the maps, and to all people who love maps

Jim West, Lakewood, Colorado

The Incredible Sinking Home

Frustration was apparent on the face of the man who asked for a map of the Commerce City area.

"A contactor built a home for me in Commerce City a few years ago," he told me, "but recently it began slowly sinking like it was built in a swamp. The contractor had no explanation. He told me it was all open land and he had just purchased and developed it. He said he had no reason to believe there was any problem.

"But my home kept sinking," he continued. "I filed suit against the contractor and I'm looking for information about what existed on this land before he built my home."

My customer and I were in luck.

Because the USGS has historically updated their maps, there is a wealth of information on how features such as buildings and roads have changed over time. I could look at earlier maps of the same area to find details which no longer exist on current maps.

I pulled a map of Commerce City and said, "Show me exactly where your home is located."

He pinpointed the location and I started looking for previous versions of the map to see what we could find. The database showed six versions of the map, the oldest from 1938.

We started by looking at a 1950 version of the map, but found nothing much different from the current edition. But when I looked at the 1938 version, I found the answer to the mysterious, sinking home.

The 1938 map showed a large gravel quarry in the exact location where my customer's home was built. We surmised that the gravel pit was abandoned sometime after 1938 and covered with fill dirt. The 1940 map showed the gravel pit but the 1947 map did not, so we were able to bracket the date when the gravel pit was filled.

Even though several decades had passed since the gravel pit was covered, the combination of fill dirt and the fluid nature of gravel had made the home site unstable.

Our research also revealed that the home site was located in the town of Derby which no longer exists. Commerce City was originally settled in 1859 and grew rapidly over the years. It was named Commerce Town until 1962 when the city annexed Derby, grew to earn city status, and changed its named to Commerce City. Derby disappeared from the next map like it had never existed.

The customer was amazed.

"I had no idea you could find such information so far in the past on a map," he said.

"I don't think the contractor knew what was under the surface and that this was once a gravel pit, but I'm sure this will help us in arriving at some settlement.

"Now that I know what is going on, I can make plans to fix the problem. Mine was the first home built in this development. I wonder if other homes in the development are also at risk of sinking. This information is invaluable to me."

Historic maps are helpful not only in settling lawsuits, but are often useful to scientists, historians, environmentalists, genealogists, and others researching a particular geographic location or area.

Unfortunately, maps don't always solve a customer's problem.

In another case, a customer asked me for information on property he had purchased near Dove Creek in Dolores County. The land was recently opened for private development. My customer had built a home with a long driveway through his property. He had fenced both sides of his driveway, his property, and home.

The following spring he found part of his fence along his driveway demolished and evidence that cattle had been driven through the fence and across his driveway. Upon investigation, he found that local ranchers had been using the route across his driveway as a cattle drive for decades.

He brought suit against the ranchers for destroying his property. But when he brought his case before the county officials, he found they were well-acquainted with the ranchers, and sympathetic to their cause. My customer lost his suit.

He came to the map store to find how long the ranchers owned the land and how long they had been using the property as a cattle route.

Sadly, in this case, the map didn't help. It did not show cattle trails nor did it show how long the ranchers owned the land.

But that didn't deter my customer from buying maps of the area to show past changes.

Historic maps continue to be an invaluable link to our collective past. My customers loved them.

The Genealogy Detective

Genealogy research has become more and more popular in the past few decades, as people search for both their roots and their fondest childhood memories.

USGS maps are a useful tool for map store customers conducting genealogy research, especially when they're searching for ancestral homes. These topographic maps have various fascinating features, including small, black squares which show every building in a rural or even uninhabited, forested area, from mountain cabins to abandoned farm buildings. This makes them beloved by people looking for their memories, memories that would never be found on any other type of map.

But getting to the map store was almost as challenging as accessing those old memories. The store was housed in building 810 on the sprawling campus of the Denver Federal Center (DFC). The main entrance to the Federal Center is on Kipling Boulevard north of Alameda Avenue, past guards who ask for your personal information and destination.

The guards usually check the visitor's driver license and let them pass. But occasionally they ask visitors to open the hood of their car to check the engine compartment. They also use a mirror to look under the car to check for explosives.

After making it successfully through the guard station, visitors had to drive through two confusing intersections, past the rear of the building and its loading docks, and around to the entrance on the west side.

So we knew anyone navigating all these obstacles was pretty determined to find a map, a map that had a strong meaning for them.

Such was the case with a distinguished looking, grey-haired, elderly gentleman who entered the store one afternoon.

"Do you have any maps of Kentucky?" he asked in a rich Southern accent.

"I have maps of the entire state," I responded. I opened the Kentucky map index and explained what maps were in it. "Just select the map you want and I'll have it brought here for you."

After a bit of looking the gentleman asked for two maps to inspect. When they arrived, he looked them over.

A bit later he said quietly, "Oh my goodness!"

I asked if he found what he was looking for. He smiled and pointed to the map. "Do you see this?" He pointed to a tiny black square on the map.

"This is the cabin that my great-grandfather built when he settled this property back in 1845. After he died, my grandfather lived here. I remember visiting him when I was a boy," His eyes were alight as he gazed at the black square. "And see this curve in the road?" He poked at a line with his forefinger. "This was called Lund's Curve because old man Lund owned the property along the curve and they named the curve after him."

The man smiled broadly as old memories came flooding back. "I'm amazed I found this cabin and that it is still on the map," he said softly. "I cannot begin to tell you the happy times I spent there, the memories…"

Now he pointed to a tiny body of water near the cabin. "That's where my Grandpa taught me to fish. That's where I went ice fishing one winter and fell right through. If not for Grandpa's black lab, I wouldn't be standing here today."

I wanted to hear more about his adventures in this cabin, but something about the look on his face stopped me from intruding. After all, there are memories we want to share and others we just want to savor for ourselves.

He looked at the map for a long time, nodding to himself, his eyes far away, before he brought it over to the counter and paid for it. He held his map and his memories tightly to his heart as he left. I couldn't help but notice his back was a bit straighter, his stride just a bit lighter than when he walked in.

One little black square on a map had brought his great-grandfather and his grandfather back to life. I'd call that priceless.

A Storied History

Few people who came to the map store were familiar with the rich and storied history of the Denver Federal Center.

In 1869, Major Jacob Downing built a ranch on property west of Kipling Boulevard. In 1913, he sold it to Thomas Hayden. In 1941, the federal government purchased a 2,100 acre parcel of the ranch to build a munitions manufacturing plant to meet the ammunition needs of World War II.

The munitions plant became the Denver Ordnance Plant (DOP) and was managed by Remington Arms until it closed in 1945. Much of the ammunition for small arms weapons used in World War II combat was produced here. At its peak of production, the DOP employed 22,000 people and manufactured 6.2 million cartridges per day.

After the war ended in 1945, the government declared the DOP and its nearly 200 buildings surplus but retained 690 acres (about one square mile) to house other government agencies. The Veterans Administration was the first to move into the old DOP buildings in 1946. It was followed by many of the federal government offices and labs housed there today, including the USGS.

During the height of the 1962 Cuban Missile Crisis, the Denver Federal Center was intended to serve as the nation's capitol in the event Washington D.C. was destroyed by a nuclear bomb. All the buildings were numbered rather than named so it would be impossible for an enemy to determine what the buildings contained.

Building 810 was built in 1963 after the crisis, and today, the building's main tenant is the USGS.

There are a couple of interesting buildings on the DFC campus. One of them is building 710. Standing in the parking lot in front of building 810 and looking directly east, map store customers saw a grass covered mound with a few antennas and exhaust pipes on the top. Driving around to the other side of the grassy mound they could see an entrance sign to building 710.

But no building is visible.

Building 710 was built with two levels below ground and today is home to the Federal Emergency Management Agency (FEMA). Completed in 1969 by the Army Corps of Engineers, it was built as a Cold War defense structure, an underground bunker designed to withstand a nuclear blast. The building was to be the base for federal operations in the event of a nuclear attack. It was designed to house 300 people for 30 days.

Originally built with male and female dormitories and medical facilities on the second level, it still houses mechanical systems, storage, offices, restrooms, a lunchroom, and a kitchen on the first level.

On August 2, 2000, the structure was added to the National Register of Historic Places for its connection to Cold War history and its architectural significance.

But most map store customers never noticed the grassy mound and knew nothing of the underground building. Before it was built, the government contracted with local ranchers and allowed goats to roam the area. The goats kept the grass clipped and the ranchers enjoyed free grazing for their goats.

Another DFC campus building that most map store customers were unaware of is the building housing the TRIGA nuclear reactor. The reactor is operated by the USGS and used for analysis and nuclear-based testing for the USGS and universities throughout the country.

Built in the late 1960's, the TRIGA reactor is similar to those at universities with their own research and training reactors. It is capable of continuous steady-state operation of 1,000 kilowatts and may be pulsed to a peak power of approximately 1,600 megawatts.

The reactor uses state-of-the-art techniques to produce nuclear changes in rocks and minerals to determine their ages. It provides high-quality data on rock and mineral composition, along with the research tools needed to develop new and improved analytical methods.

A drive along the north or east side of the DFC will reveal two large solar arrays which supply power to the federal center. Additional solar arrays are located on the roof of building 810.

A small, rarely visited, one-room museum in the General Services Administration building tells the Federal Center Story.

The most recent changes to the DFC campus include the annexation of the west side by Jefferson County to build a new St. Anthony's Hospital. It is also a stop for the West Line of the Denver Regional Transportation District Light Rail.

The Ladies from La Junta

I was always intrigued by people's connection to a particular place, the memories it stirred up, and how something as simple as looking at a location on a map could evoke such strong emotions.

One day two women entered the store. An elderly Hispanic lady, stooped and unsteady with age, leaned heavily on the arm of a dark-haired, younger woman whom I later learned was her daughter.

The daughter said she was doing genealogy research and wanted a map of the area where her family had lived when she was a young child.

"We have maps of all parts of Colorado. Where are you from?"

She told me as a child, they'd lived near La Junta in the southeastern part of Colorado but didn't know exactly where because her family moved when she was quite young. "Do you remember anything that could help the man find the right map Mama?" the daughter asked her mother.

Her mother shook her head, looking down, but I thought I saw sadness in her eyes and the set of her lips. I wondered what the circumstances of their leaving La Junta might have been.

As with all customers who came to the store looking for a location they weren't quite sure of, this turned into a kind of detective game. I asked the ladies from La Junta a series of questions.

"How far from La Junta did you live?"

"I'm not sure, maybe about five or six miles," the daughter said.

"What direction from town?"

The daughter conferred briefly with her mother. "East."

"Did the road from town go straight to your house or did you have to make any turns?"

"We made one turn to the right, then another turn to the right to enter our driveway."

"How far between turns?"

"I'm not sure, maybe two or three miles."

The old lady remained silent. I felt her interest in the discussion along with something else, some emotion churning inside her.

"Did you like living in that area?" I wasn't prying, just making conversation as I looked through the maps, searching for the one that matched their information.

The old lady spoke to me for the first time. "Yes, we loved it there." She nodded and a bit of wetness gleamed in her eyes. I could tell that home, that area, or perhaps that particular time in her life meant a lot to her.

Little by little we narrowed down the location until I was able to find a 7 ½ minute quadrangle topographic map that showed the general area where the ladies once lived.

A 7 ½ minute quadrangle map, often called a quad or topo, refers to a specific map size. Unlike your average street map, a quad is printed in degrees of latitude and longitude.

Latitude is measured in degrees starting with zero degrees at the equator. There are 90 degrees of latitude north of the equator to the North Pole and 90 degrees south of the equator to the South Pole.

Latitude lines are also called parallels. Baseline road in Boulder is exactly 40 degrees north of the equator and is therefore referred to as the 40th parallel.

Longitude lines, also called meridians, run perpendicular to latitude and run through both poles. There is no obvious zero point for longitude, so by international agreement, Greenwich, England, was chosen as zero degrees longitude. This meridian is referred to as the prime meridian.

The earth is divided equally into 360 degrees of longitude, which makes perfect sense if you consider that a circle—the earth—is 360 degrees. There are

180 degrees east of the prime meridian and 180 degrees west of the prime meridian.

Degrees of latitude and longitude are further divided into minutes and seconds: there are 60 minutes in one degree and 60 seconds in one minute.

Therefore, the quad map at Baseline road in Boulder would begin at a latitude of 40 degrees and end at 40 degrees, 7 minutes and 30 seconds. The longitude of the map would also be 7 ½ minutes which is why it is called a 7 ½ minute map.

A quad map at the equator is square. But as you move north or south of the equator, the longitude lines converge and the maps become narrower. That is why Colorado quads are not as wide as they are tall. A 7 ½ minute map in Colorado covers about 6 ½ miles horizontally and 8 ½ miles vertically.

These maps also have contour lines showing the elevations and the topography (forests, streams, mountains, and other geographical features) of the areas on the map. Hence the nickname topo map.

But the ladies from La Junta were not interested in all that detail. They merely stared down at the map, the mother clutching her daughter's arm.

"Did you have a long driveway with your house in the middle of a large circle at the end?" I asked.

With this both women looked at me wide-eyed. "How did you know about the circle?" the daughter asked.

"Because it's here on the map," I said. They both looked more closely at the map then looked at me with big smiles.

"I can't believe you found our house," the daughter said. "Thank you so much!

"Remember Mama? The school bus used to stop on the road at the end of our driveway because there wasn't enough room for the bus to turn around in our yard in front of our house. We had to walk about one-half mile down the road to meet the bus.

"One day the county sent a road grader that plowed a big circle around our house. That way, the bus could pick us up, circle around the back of our house, and drive back to the road. After that we never had to walk the half-mile to the road. I'm surprised that road is on this map!"

The ladies spent more time examining the map, pointing to landmarks they remembered in the area. They found a stock tank and a small stream that ran behind their former house, and told me they used to raise cattle that used the stock tank for water.

"What do you think, Mama? Would you like to take a drive down there one day?"

The elderly lady's face lit up and a broad smile crept over her face. "I would like that very much."

The daughter bought the map and they left, arm in arm, with their new treasure. I was happy to have helped them rediscover their old home and the many clearly happy memories that went with it.

I never did find out the circumstances that caused them to leave La Junta.

Death on Needle Mountain

The Wind River Mountains in Wyoming are aptly named.

The range lies at an angle pointing northwest, directly into the wind that barrels over the Tetons and across the plains. Storms build rapidly in these mountains and descend on them with unbridled fury. As I had recently returned from a backpacking trip there, I knew firsthand the Winds' extreme weather as well as the rugged terrain.

So when a slender, middle-aged man asked for a map of Needle Mountain near Big Sandy Lake, I knew right where to look. But although the maps I checked showed the mountains in the Big Sandy area, I could not find Needle Mountain. I checked the USGS website for Needle Mountain in Wyoming but found no entries with that name.

The customer and I examined the map closely. He pointed out an unnamed needle-shaped peak which he thought was the mountain he was looking for. He told me it was known by the locals as Needle Mountain, although it was not officially named on the map.

That could easily be the case; there are thousands of peaks in the Mountain West which are not named.

"Do you know why I am looking for this peak?" he asked softly.

"No, I don't," I said. It wasn't until then that I looked closely at his face and saw it was lined with grief.

His pain was apparent, and his eyes filled with tears as he told me his story.

"Four years ago my son and his girlfriend climbed this peak. It is a technical climb and they used ropes to belay each other as they ascended. As they reached the summit, the weather worsened quickly and a severe lightning storm approached.

"They decided to descend to a cleft in the mountain a bit below them to get some protection from the coming storm and the rain that was beginning to fall. After they were safely in the cleft, my son noticed that their climbing rope was still hanging down the side of the mountain and was getting wet."

His voice trembled as he continued his tale.

"He felt that if lightning struck, the rope could act like a conduit to him. So he reached out to retrieve the rope. As he did, lightning struck him and he died instantly.

He was 21 years old."

I looked at him in disbelief.

"I am so sorry," was all I could think to say, but my heart went out to him.

"His girlfriend then had the terrible task of descending this peak alone, without help from my son. She made it down without incident, then hiked out to the trailhead to call for help. She waited until the rescue team arrived and guided them back to the peak to retrieve my son's body.

"I want to hike to this peak to get some closure," he said.

We stood together for long time looking at the map, his eyes vacant and his thoughts far away with his son on the mountain in Wyoming.

Suddenly an idea came to mind and I said, "If this peak is unnamed, perhaps there may be a way to have it named for your son."

Returning to the present, he looked at me with interest and I went on to tell him about the Geographic Name Information Service (GNIS) website which is the source of all names on all USGS topo maps.

Together we went to the map store computer, looked online at the GNIS website and found an application form to name a peak.

We examined the form and I helped him with the geographic location of the peak and some tips on how to fill out the form.

He seemed pleased with the idea and said he would go home, print out the form, fill it out and send it in.

He left with the map, seemingly somewhat happier than when he first came in.

It was all I could do to comfort him.

Sometimes that is enough.

I never heard if he was successful in getting "Needle Mountain" named for his son.

I hope he was.

The Four Passes Hike

Colorado is known for the Rocky Mountains and the über-fit outdoor enthusiasts who play in them. And sometimes the play can be pretty intense. Trail running, mountain biking, camping and backpacking, rappelling, cliff climbing—if it's humanly possible, you'll find humans who love to try it. For this type of mountain lover, no amount of exertion is too much.

Not even the exertion needed for the "four passes" hike. This arduous experience starts southwest of Aspen near Maroon Lake, elevation 9,800 feet. The trail ascends Buckskin Pass, Trail Rider Pass, Frigid Air Pass, and West Maroon Pass for a total elevation gain of over 7,600 feet. The trip is more than 27 miles, and is usually done in two or three days with a backpack. At higher elevations approaching the passes, the trail is steep, rocky and traverses several tricky-to-navigate boulder fields.

There are a few stream crossings, easily navigated when water levels are low. But when the mountain runoff is heavy, it's necessary to ford these streams at higher water levels.

It's a strenuous trip, and with much of the trail above tree line over 11,000 feet, the going is slow. I feel tired just thinking about it. But others have a different opinion.

One early summer day an attractive young woman wearing a T-shirt and shorts came in to the map store asking for maps of the "four passes" hike. Her toned muscles said she was an athlete, obviously fit and strong. Together we looked at several Trails Illustrated maps until we found the route over the four passes.

After years of hiking and backpacking in the Colorado Rockies, I have a good sense of how long it takes to hike over the state's high altitude passes. "How many days are you planning on for this hike?"

Her eyebrow arched and one corner of her lip quirked upward. "I expect to do the entire trip in six to eight hours."

"Six hours!" I think my jaw might have dropped. "How can you do all that mileage and elevation in only six hours?"

"I'm a trail runner. I run the entire length. The current record is four hours and 27 minutes, held by a professional runner." Her tone was confident and excited.

I was dumbfounded, but I shouldn't have been. The ranks of trail runners increase annually. Between 2006 and 2012 they grew from 4.5 million to more than 6 million in the United States alone. Accordingly, the number of organized trail races has grown over the past few years throughout the world. Today it is now well into the hundreds in North America alone.

Trail runners often cite less joint impact stress compared to road running. They prefer a non-urban environment. Competitions in non-traditional, off-road triathlons and adventure racing have also increased over the past five years.

I asked her to tell me how she does it.

"I run uphill as long as I can until I get winded. Then I walk for a bit to catch my breath, and run again until I can't run any longer. When I get to the top of the pass, I stop for a brief rest and wait for my friends. Usually about six or eight of us run as a group. When everyone catches up, we run downhill to the bottom and start all over again going up to the next pass."

The level of fitness required to do this is truly astonishing. "Do you carry any rain gear?"

"I carry an ultra-light rain jacket. It's not completely waterproof, but our body heat keeps us warm. Our trail running shoes don't have the traction you hikers have with hiking boots, but they have a nylon insole to protect our feet from the sharp rocks."

"You need this particular map for a run like that."

She shook her head. "We don't carry maps. I'll memorize the trail from this map before I run."

Now I was really impressed. "I can see why you'd want to carry as little as possible. But what if you get injured from a fall or a twisted ankle? What if the temperature drops dramatically?"

"We don't carry extra food or clothing or a first-aid kit. If someone gets hurt, the first person to finish the run tells a support group at the trailhead and they go back with first-aid gear and more clothing if needed."

"You must carry food and water."

"Yes, two to three liters of water and a few trail snacks in my hydration pack to maintain my energy on the run."

"This is amazing. How do you feel at the end of one of these runs?"

She laughed. "Exhausted. I guzzle gallons of water and eat something right away because I'm so depleted. But by the next weekend I'm ready to do it all over again. We do a run like this every weekend if our schedules permit."

She bought the maps and all but bounded out the door. I was fascinated by the different approaches we all take to communing with the Rockies and exploring Colorado's high passes.

But after hearing about her approach, I think I will stay with mine. Slow and easy is how I win my races.

Bounty Hunter

Being a student of human nature, I often played a little mental game where I tried to guess why customers wanted a map just by looking at them.

If people looked fit and strong, as if they could carry a pack to the top of a high peak without breaking a sweat, I expected them to be hikers looking for trail maps.

If someone walked in wearing a camouflage hat, asking for a map identifying public from private land, that was a no brainer. Obviously a hunter.

But this guy kept me guessing.

He looked like a former marine drill sergeant or perhaps a law enforcement officer. In his fifties, he was built like a bull terrier, with salt and pepper hair and beard cut short.

"Got any maps of Arizona?" he asked in a gravelly voice.

"Certainly. What part of Arizona?"

"South Central, on the border with Mexico."

We looked at an Arizona index and after a few minutes he decided on a 100,000 scale Bureau of Land Management map.

Map scales tell the user how detailed a map is. For example, a 1:24,000 scale map contains much more detail than a 1:100,000 scale map. On a 1:24,000 scale map, one mile on the ground is shown as about two and one-half inches on the map. On a 1:100,000 scale map, one mile on the ground is shown as about one-half inch on the map. The detail, therefore, must be much less.

I retrieved the map and he carefully looked it over.

He pointed to an area near the border. "See this? These are arroyos that run from Arizona south to Mexico. Do you know what they're for?"

"Illegal immigration routes?" I guessed.

"Some of that, but mostly drug cartels use them for smuggling drugs into the U.S."

Now my curiosity was really piqued. "What kind of work do you do?"

"I'm a bounty hunter."

I'd never met a bounty hunter before and asked him to tell me more.

"I'll give you an example," he said. "Earlier this year the sheriff in Greeley contacted me about a woman he'd arrested and later set free on $10,000 bail. She jumped bail and the sheriff suspected she had headed for her home in Mexico. He asked me if

I'd try to bring her back. So I headed for Buena Vista, a small town near the Arizona border. I hired a *coyote* to find her in Mexico and bring her back."

A coyote is a local Mexican who knows the area and brings people across the border illegally.

He continued. "A few days later I got a call from the coyote telling me that he'd found the woman, detained her, and would meet me in Buena Vista to hand her over. I picked her up from the coyote, put her in my car and drove her back to Greeley. I handed her over to the sheriff who then promptly stuck her back in jail. Then I headed for the bail bondsman to collect my fee."

Pursuing criminals as a bounty hunter can be a dangerous business. Many bounty hunters carry a weapon, mace or a gun, but according to this gentleman, the most valuable weapon is the element of surprise. Violence is not the norm because the most violent criminals are not let out on bail and because most criminals don't put up a fight when they are apprehended. Usually less than five percent resist arrest by a bounty hunter.

Not like what you see on TV at all.

He chuckled. "It's quite interesting work. Would you like to come along on my next trip?"

"Thanks but no thanks." We both laughed.

I couldn't imagine myself dealing with coyotes or runaway prisoners.

Antarctica

The map store sold many specialty maps. For example, Earth at Night, a satellite picture of the earth showing lights of populated areas. Or the U.S. in 1857 showing the states and territories existing at that time. Another specialty map featured Colorado in 1894 showing rail lines and towns of that day, many of which are now ghost towns. A Civil War map showing battles and troop movements was very popular. As were maps of Antarctica.

Why people wanted them or what they did with them was a bit of a mystery, but Antarctica maps were in greater demand than I would have guessed. So I wasn't surprised when a stocky, gray-haired fellow with a military bearing and bright blue eyes came into the store and asked for a map of a mountainous region in west central Antarctica.

I ordered the map brought up from the warehouse and while we were waiting, asked him why he was interested in this particular area of Antarctica.

"I want to see if the map shows the mountain named after me," he said.

As you might imagine, that got my attention. "Why do you have a mountain named after you?"

"In the 1950s, the USGS was doing aerial mapping of the continent. I flew one of the planes that made repeated passes over this area taking photos of the mountains. The USGS developed the film and made maps of the continent."

My impression that he had a military bearing had not been far off. He had the intelligent look and clear, keen eyes of a former pilot.

"So the USGS named the mountain after you because you flew the plane when the photos were taken?"

"That's right. The USGS needed names for all the mountains in the area, so they used my name and the names of the other crew members. We thought these names were only temporary, but I understand they became permanent and still exist today."

"That must have been incredible."

"You have no idea. The vastness and isolation and the beauty of that area, well, it's like nothing you can even imagine. I felt like a true explorer, an adventurer."

When the map arrived from the warehouse, we unrolled it. He bent his head and studied the mountain range clearly visible on the map.

"Here it is." He looked up at me with a jubilant grin, pointing at the mountain that bore his name.

"Here is the mountain named after me, and these mountains are named after the crew." He pointed out mountains named after the photographer, the navigator, the co-pilot, and other crew members. There were also mountains named after the pilot and crews of other planes that had participated in the aerial mapping of the area.

"I can't wait to show this to my grandkids. They don't really believe there's a mountain named after me. Heck, I wasn't sure I believed it anymore myself." He grinned as the memories came flooding back and he relived the flights he made over the rugged and desolate mountains of Antarctica. A place on this earth that few have ever seen in person nor are likely to ever see.

After he left I spent some time looking at Antarctica maps, imagining how it must have felt to fly over the trackless waste, insulated from the dangerous environment by several tons of metal, creating maps for the world to see. I wished he would have stayed a bit longer and talked more about his experiences.

That was one of the odd things about working for the map store. Each customer and each map had a story attached, something meaningful and even profound. But although I helped them find their maps, I usually had to be content with only a smidgeon of the story.

Fifty Square Miles per Quad

August, September, and October found the map store crowded with hunters.

A few came from out of state carrying their rifles with them as they stopped at the Federal Center on their way to the areas they planned to hunt.

But the guards at the entrance gate had other ideas.

Hunters were not allowed to bring their rifles on the Federal Center. Nor were they allowed to leave their rifles in the waiting area near the guard station while they looked at maps.

The guards' suggestion? Rent a hotel room and leave the guns in the room until they bought their maps. And that is what many had to do.

The hunters frequently gave me the number of the hunt management unit they had drawn and wanted all the maps covering those hunting units.

Invariably, they underestimated the size of the hunt unit and the area they planned to hunt.

Hunt management units are usually covered by some or all of one or more Bureau of Land Management (BLM) maps and each BLM map is comprised of 32 7 ½ minute maps.

I would ask where in the unit they intended to hunt, to narrow down their hunt area to a realistic size and concentrate their efforts on a smaller part with the best chance for hunt success.

When hunters said that they planned to hunt the entire unit, I knew they had no idea what this meant. This was the case when three middle-aged men decked out in full hunting gear showed up one fall day. Their gear looked brand new and their expectations looked to be high.

"Show us all the maps of this area," one of the men said. He showed me the unit they planned to hunt. It covered most of a BLM map.

"We've seen some big elk in this area," the second man said.

"What part of the unit do you intend to hunt? I asked.

"The entire unit," they replied.

I decided to give them more information about the size of a hunt unit. "See this little cross on the BLM map?" I asked.

"Yes, what is it?" The first guy leaned in.

"That's a corner of a 7 ½ minute quad map. As you can see, there are lots of these map corners on the BLM map. In fact there are 32 quad maps on this larger BLM map."

"So?" he asked. I got one of the quad maps from the shelves to explain further. Using the map's contour lines I showed him the features of the terrain he might be hunting, pointing out the hill tops, valleys, meadows and wooded areas. He was impressed with the level of detail. The other two became more interested.

Then I came to the point of my exercise. "Do you know how many square miles are on this one quad map?"

"I have no idea." The first hunter's eyes narrowed. He was starting to see what I was getting at.

"There are over 55 square miles on this one quad map, and there are 32 of these quad maps on the BLM map. That means there are over 1,700 square miles on the BLM map. Do you plan to hunt the entire 1,700 square miles?"

Three heads swiveled in my direction, three pairs of eyes widened, and three men rapidly began revising their expectations and plans. They suddenly realized they could never hunt 1,700 square miles on a single trip.

In fact, this information was usually news even to veteran hunters. Once they learned how much territory a single 7 ½ minute quad covered, they often said they'd have to do some scouting and pre-trip planning to find the best areas to hunt.

"Maybe one of these quad maps is all we need," they finally said.

"Do your maps show us where the elk are," the third man asked.

"Our maps don't show elk concentrations, I said. "'But you can find summer and winter elk locations as well as migration routes on the Colorado Parks and Wildlife website. In fact one customer showed me on a map a south-facing ridge near a lake where he would always find elk. Unfortunately, it's not in your hunt unit."

The question remained—which one map would lead to a successful hunt? I couldn't tell them for sure where the game was. But I helped narrow down their hunt areas to give them the best chance for finding the animals they sought.

I hope they were successful.

Black Powder Moose Hunter

Hunters almost always asked for BLM maps. Of all the maps in the store, they most clearly showed land ownership. Private lands are indicated in white, state lands in blue, and federal lands in tan.

State and federal lands often include small parcels of private land, and large tracts of private land sometimes include small parcels of state and federal land.

Part of my job was to help my hunters understand this so they would know which parts of their hunting unit were on private land (where it was illegal to hunt) and which were on public land (where they were permitted to hunt).

Hunters came in all ages, but most were middle aged, so it came as a bit of a surprise when a small, wiry, elderly man with a head of unruly white hair asked me one day for a BLM map in a hunting unit in the Walden area.

"What are you hunting?"

"Moose," he answered.

He was robust and energetic and appeared to be quite spry. But it was apparent to me that he was much older than my usual hunter customer. My curiosity about his age got the best of me.

"How old are you?"

"I'm eighty years young."

He was the first eighty-year-old moose hunter I had ever met, and I was sure he had a story to tell.

"Have you ever shot a moose?"

"Yes. I shot one last year in this area during the muzzle-loading season and I'm trying for number two this year."

"Muzzle loading?" I was surprised. "Don't you need to get close when you hunt with a muzzle loading gun?"

"Yes, most animals are taken within 50 to 150 yards because muzzle loaders use iron sights. It takes lots of practice to be accurate over 150 yards."

I was duly impressed.

Muzzle loaders are the type of guns which were used in the Civil War. To load them you pour gunpowder in the barrel. You then wrap a ball in a cloth patch and push it down the barrel until it is firmly seated against the powder.

In early versions of this gun, a primer powder was poured into a "pan" and a spark produced from a piece of flint striking steel would ignite the primer.

The primer would in turn ignite the powder in the barrel to fire the gun. Occasionally, the primer would ignite, but would not ignite the black powder in the barrel. This gave rise to the expression "flash in the pan."

Modern versions use a percussion cap as a primer instead of loose primer powder which makes the ignition process more reliable.

My eighty-year-old hunter seemed to be tilting the odds in favor of the moose with his choice of arms. Hunters with a modern rifle and telescopic sight can easily take down a moose at twice the distance he could with his muzzle loader.

Having encountered moose at close range, I know they are dangerous. While hiking in Alaska a few years ago, I encountered a moose with her calf on the trail. The moose became protective and charged me. I narrowly escaped injury by throwing myself under the low hanging limbs of a nearby spruce tree.

"When you shot the moose last year, how did you get it out?"

"The hard part was walking in hip boots through a swampy area choked with willows. But I walked back to my truck, drove down the road and got as near to the moose as I could. I tied one end of a rope to the moose antlers and the other end to my truck and slowly dragged the moose through the willows to the edge of the road.

"Then I drove down the road and enlisted the help of some nearby hunters to load the moose onto my truck. They were happy to help."

He smiled, obviously proud of his accomplishment.

I could see why. I wished him good luck as he headed off to the hunt.

School Tours

School tours were always an interesting part of working in the map store. Elementary schools brought busloads of kids to the Federal Center for tours of the USGS. They toured the enormous warehouse which stored millions of maps, the rock and ice core lab, and of course, the map store.

The USGS map warehouse was impressive in its size and scope. It was over two acres in size, and stored more than 20 million maps on the shelves, including roughly 60,000 7 ½ minute map titles. It also held thousands of larger maps and technical publications covering hundreds of geologic subjects and over 100,000 other products.

The warehouse was also a shipping and distribution center that sent maps to map stores throughout the country. It was always a beehive of activity with people retrieving maps from shelves for the map store or for shipping to some distant retail outlet. Visitors never failed to be impressed.

Elementary school students were well behaved when they first came in. Although the teachers did their best to maintain order, it didn't take long for the high-energy kids to get out of hand.

Because a few of our maps were large, we rolled them into a tube and placed them in a plastic sleeve for protection. The kids, of course, saw these long tubes as swords and light sabers and loved having mock sword fights with them.

The many large animal hand puppets we stocked were especially popular and the kids loved playing with them, talking in strange voices to imitate the animals. Our stuffed birds played recorded bird songs when a pressure spot on the bird's back was pressed. When 15 or 20 kids picked up these birds and pressed their backs to start the bird calls, the map store was filled with a cacophony of bird sounds.

We always tried to engage the kids by showing them the different kinds of maps and other various items we offered for sale to the general public. They were especially interested in the raised relief maps and would run their little fingers over the mountains in delight.

On the other hand, when we discussed the concept behind topography and how topographic lines represented mountains and valleys, we were usually met with blank stares.

School Tours

The USGS had a large waiting area with a few interactive demonstrations for visitors. The most popular was a pressure-sensitive pad connected to a computer monitor. It showed pressure on the pad as seismic activity. When you stepped on the pad a line on the monitor spiked up. The harder the pressure, the higher the spike.

It didn't take long for the kids to realize that if they jumped up and down on the pad they would see a series of sharp spikes in the line on the monitor. Soon a dozen or more kids were pushing and shoving each other to get their chance to jump on the pad to see who could make the highest spike.

High school students were entirely different. They were mostly bored with the entire tour, or at least that's how they acted. We valiantly tried to interest them in maps with little success.

Only a few were fascinated with topographic maps and they flooded us with questions, eager to learn more.

School tours included a trip to the ice core lab. The USGS and other scientific organizations drill cores in the Arctic and Antarctic ice and send these cores to the ice core lab. Scientists in the lab analyze the cores to gather information on many things, including past climate changes.

Although their teachers usually explained the environment of the ice core lab in advance, few students dressed for the sub-freezing temperatures in the lab. Ice cores are stored in a huge walk-in freezer. The students went inside for a short discussion of ice core technology. When they came shivering back to the map store, we enjoyed making it a point to ask them what they thought about the ice core lab.

Working with young people was always fun. There was never a dull moment when they came to visit.

We loved school tours.

Christmas and a
Handmade Relief Map

Christmas was always a special time at the map store. We decorated the store with paper snowflakes hung from the ceiling and put up a Christmas tree decorated with lights, ornaments, and garlands. Packages wrapped in maps instead of Christmas paper lay under the tree.

But the highlight of the season was the "map wrapping paper" giveaway.

Every year we rolled up maps and secured each roll with a rubber band. Hundreds of these rolled maps were placed on a table covered with a festive red cloth to give away as Christmas wrapping paper.

People loved the idea of using maps to wrap Christmas gifts and would come from miles away to pick them up. We gave away hundreds of rolled maps each holiday season.

We sent press releases to all the local TV stations, to the Denver Post Hub newspapers and to numerous smaller local newspapers. Not all would use the press release, but when they did, even a shortened version, people would find the announcement, walk into the map store clutching the tiny clipping and ask for the free map wrapping paper.

We limited our giveaway to two rolls per customer to ensure that all customers would get the maps they wanted. One woman asked if she could have more than two rolls. I asked if she had a lot of wrapping to do. She said no, she intended to wallpaper her bathroom with the maps and two rolls weren't enough. She planned to apply wallpaper paste, glue odd shaped pieces of maps to the walls and seal the maps with clear varnish. I thought this was such a fabulous idea, I relented and gave her four rolls, all the maps she needed to redecorate her bathroom.

The free map wrapping paper was a big hit and drew hundreds of new customers to the map store. I remember one woman who stopped dead in her tracks when she came in. She saw the colorful displays, the animal hand puppets, and racks of books, and threw open her arms in surprise exclaiming, "Who knew?"

During one Christmas season, an old man came in slowly pushing a walker. He looked at least 90.

Following him was his son who carefully set a cardboard box on one of the tables.

The old man asked for a list of all the peaks in Colorado, their altitude, and their location in latitude and longitude. I told him we didn't have any such list, but he was adamant, insisting that he got a list exactly like that from the USGS in the past.

"When did you get this list?" I asked him.

"Hmm. Must have been around 1930 or so."

I told him the list was probably discontinued and didn't exist today. To my relief, he didn't seem disappointed and said it wasn't important. He just wanted to see if the list still existed.

Then he asked me if I wanted to see what he brought in his box, which of course I did.

"This is a map of Coal Creek canyon." He lifted the lid off the box.

Inside was a handmade, raised relief map of the canyon with layers of what appeared to be thin cardboard.

The vast majority of the maps we sold were topographic which use contour lines to show terrain features. We had a few raised relief maps in the store, but they were machine made from pressed plastic.

His map was an incredible piece of art which showed terrain features in three dimensions, so you could easily see the mountains and valleys of Coal Creek Canyon.

I asked him how he made the map.

"I took a USGS 7 ½ minute map and traced each contour line on a piece of suit cardboard. Years ago, when you bought a suit, it was packaged in a cardboard box, and that cardboard was the perfect thickness to layer each contour."

The result was beautiful. Each contour was carefully cut out and layered on the one below it so that it perfectly matched the USGS 7 ½ minute quad.

The terrain where trees grew was painted green. The rest of the land was brown. Coal creek was a vibrant blue line.

"When did you make the map?" I asked.

"1932."

I asked if he had made any other maps like this and he said no, they just took too much time.

We looked at the fine detail. Everyone in the store came over and marveled at the workmanship, discussing the amount of time it must have taken him to cut out all the cardboard pieces and carefully place them to duplicate the USGS quad.

I think he enjoyed all the attention he was getting. I was extremely interested and impressed.

This delightful man had come a long way to show off his beautiful shaded relief map—his labor of love.

Alaska

Alaska is enormous. More than 586,400 square miles in size, it has over 3,000 rivers, 29 volcanoes, 100,000 glaciers, 33,000 miles of coastline, and over three million lakes, mostly unnamed.

So when I was asked to find one specific unnamed lake I knew I had my work cut out for me.

The dark-haired, middle-aged man looking for this unnamed Alaskan lake knew its approximate location but little else. And we carried over 100 detailed maps covering the state.

The map store brought in many visitors looking for Alaska maps. Because most people had a specific destination or location in mind, I could usually find what they were looking for. I knew how to conduct a routine search but this promised to be anything but routine. So I decided to find out what was so important about this particular lake.

"Are you planning a fishing trip to the area?"

"No, I am not planning a vacation trip." A cloud of sadness passed over his face.

"Many years ago, when I was in graduate school, my professor took a small group of his students to this lake to camp and spend a week studying the evolutionary biology of large North American mammals — grizzly, black bear, wolves, and moose.

"We had to fly in to the lake, but all of us and our gear would not fit on one plane. So our professor sent us ahead with some of our gear. He was to follow on the next plane with the remaining bulk of the gear.

"We flew to this absolutely beautiful remote lake, unloaded our gear, and the plane turned around and flew back to pick up our professor. We set up camp at the edge of the lake and waited.

But the plane with our professor didn't come.

We assumed there was some reason the plane was unable to return that day and expected it would show up the following morning.

"There we were at this remote lake, all alone, without our trusted professor. None of us was experienced at wilderness survival and our anxiety grew as darkness fell. Knowing about the wolves and bears we had come to study, we were quite apprehensive. We built a fire, cooked dinner, and kept up a nervous conversation. We tried to ignore all the sounds in the nearby forest, sure that a bear or pack of wolves would attack at any minute.

"Eventually we climbed exhausted into our sleeping bags.

"The next morning, there was still no sign of a plane or our professor. Although our anxiety was turning to concern, we maintained hope that perhaps the pilot was again unable to make the return flight that day and would surely come the following day. We had no radio or other means of communication with our professor or the pilot so had no alternative but to wait and hope they would come.

"We had enough gear and food to last several days, but the gear we needed to conduct our studies was coming with our professor. Every time we heard the distant sound of a plane our hopes soared. But no plane came. We spent another fitful night alone at our camp sure that the plane with our professor and gear would show up the next morning. But the next day there was still no sign of them. Now we were genuinely worried.

"Finally, after three fretful days a plane crested the distant ridge heading straight for us. Our relief was tangible. The plane landed and taxied to our campsite. Eagerly we ran toward it to greet our professor and help unload the equipment. But the plane was empty except for the pilot, and not the same pilot who'd flown us in and who we expected to fly our professor in.

"The pilot emerged from the cockpit and told us the story we did not want to hear. The plane with our professor on board had developed engine trouble on its return flight and crashed in a heavily wooded wilderness area, killing all on board.

"Our professor and all our gear were gone." At this point my customer turned his face away. I stayed quiet, waiting. Finally he looked up at me and continued.

"We couldn't believe it. With heavy hearts we broke camp, packed up our gear and loaded it on the plane. Then, with a last look around, we climbed aboard and flew back to Anchorage. None of us have been back since."

I was speechless.

Sorrow blanketed his face as he spoke about this devastating incident all these years later.

"So that's why I'm looking for that lake. I'm putting together a return trip for those of us who were on that original trip. We want to go back and find some closure. I need to do this for my own peace of mind."

So we put our heads together and retraced his route from Anchorage. He remembered they'd headed almost due north toward the Brooks Range. He estimated the distance and I checked the database for maps of the area.

After some searching we found a lake that looked promising and I produced a map for him to see. He examined the map carefully, spotted some familiar lakes and terrain features.

"Yes, I believe this is the correct map." He thanked me profusely and bought the map.

I wondered how visiting the scene of this former tragedy would help any of them after so many years, or would it only bring back more painful memories.

Regardless of the outcome, I didn't envy him his melancholy trip back.

Gold Seeker

Colorado has a rich and colorful history of gold and silver miners and the lure of "striking it rich" has not changed over time. The rising price of gold brought many to the map store. They were after one of the many books and maps about the history of Colorado's gold and silver mining.

One particular specialty map showing the location of Colorado's gold and silver resources was always a best seller and tough to keep in stock. Gold and silver mines were named on the map along with historic gold-bearing streams, so it was a good resource for treasure hunters.

I always looked forward to the summer surge of gold-seekers. They were a fun, sometimes intense, wildly optimistic bunch, all convinced they were about to strike it rich on their next foray.

One young man came into the map store with surprising regularity looking for maps that showed the same thing—where he could find gold. He never had much money and could only afford to buy one or two maps at a time.

"Gold is selling for over $1,000 an ounce," he told me once. "If I could find only an ounce of gold I would have it made."

I didn't want to burst his golden bubble, so I never pointed out that in today's economy, $1,000 would not go very far. I also never told him that I had panned for gold in Colorado streams. After hours of panning, I had only found two or three nuggets, pebbles really, so tiny their weight would not even register on a scale. So gathering an ounce would be a daunting task for my young would-be gold miner.

With each visit, he diligently studied BLM maps and National Forest Service maps looking for public land where he could begin his search. I helped him find small streams and tributaries where he could pan for gold.

"I am looking for placer gold," he explained. "It's usually found in the gravel of small streams. I'm not interested in digging into a hillside trying to find a vein of gold."

On his next visit, he hadn't found a speck of gold or lost an ounce of determination.

"Show me another map," he said.

So I did. "Hey, do you know how to stake a claim if you did find gold?" I asked him.

He looked surprised. "No, I never thought about that."

I directed him to the local BLM or Forest Service regional office and to other businesses that had books and specialized equipment for finding placer gold.

Although I was skeptical he would strike it rich, I was really rooting for him.

The last time I saw this young man, he asked for maps of Alaska. He'd recently heard there was more gold in Alaska than in Colorado and that it was easier to find. At that point, I started wondering just how serious he was. Would he really head up to Alaska? If he could hardly afford the maps, how could he afford a trip to Alaska?

Months later, a colleague told me that this aspiring gold miner never made it to Alaska. He'd come in looking for maps of Nevada, having heard about the gold deposits in the Nevada mountains.

To my knowledge this young man never found gold and never became rich panning for placer gold.

We never saw him again. But what did that mean? Had he finally given up the search as futile?

Or perhaps,—unbeknownst to any of us skeptics at the map store,—had this young man's dreams finally come true?

Stranger Danger

After the 9-11 attack on the Twin Towers, like everyone else, we were told "if you see something, say something." But that is easier said than done and deciding when to say something depends on what you see and how you interpret it.

When two bearded, young, Middle Eastern men walked into the map store soon after that awful day, we treated them as regular customers. We had no reason not to. I asked if I could be of help.

"No, we're just looking around," one replied. "We're interested in maps."

And that's exactly what they did. They looked around the store at the maps, the books, and all the other items we sold.

Then one of the men wandered down the hall back toward the USGS offices and the other wandered toward the USGS offices in the other direction. Both areas were off limits to walk-in visitors. I called them back and asked them where they were going.

"We are looking for the office of the Denver director of the USGS to apply for a job. What is his name?"

Was there something about his expression, something false in his reply that gave me pause, or was I just being paranoid because of recent upsetting events?

"If you are looking for a job, your first step is to look on the Internet at usajobs.gov," I said. "That website helps you match your job skills with available jobs. When you find opportunities that interest you, you can call the contact listed and set an appointment."

As I was explaining the website one of the men wandered away again, this time heading toward the warehouse, another area forbidden to unescorted visitors. Again I called him back to the store. Something clearly was not right. I called Roland, the store manager, and told him what was happening.

Our strange visitors kept prodding me for information.

"Where is the office of your security director?" There was nothing casual about his voice.

Or was I just imagining that?

The hair on the back of my neck prickled. "You said you came in here to look at maps. Why do you need to know about the director of security?" I began wondering if they were armed.

I couldn't get a direct answer. Roland had seen enough and he called the Federal Center police. Moments later, they showed up, took control of the situation, and began questioning the two men.

They clearly didn't like the answers they were getting and escorted the two men off the Federal Center campus. We were told to call immediately if the men ever came back and also if anything unusual occurred.

After this episode we were all on heightened alert and speculating what the two men were up to. Were they maybe scouting the USGS building to determine the level of security to plan some future attack? Were they aware of the building with the hidden bunker or the nuclear reactor?

I have to admit I was jumpy, checking out every customer a bit more carefully for quite a while after that. But the whole country was jumpy. It was a scary and uncertain time for all of us.

We never saw those two men again, but the incident made us more aware of potential danger.

And we were glad we said something when we saw something.

Summer Snowstorm

Colorado has 54 peaks rising over 14,000 feet in altitude. Most of these "fourteeners" require climbing 3,000 feet or more in elevation and several miles in distance to reach the summit. Some peaks are relatively easy with well-traveled trails to the summits. But others are quite difficult with loose rocks and steep drops where just one misstep can be fatal.

Despite the dangers, Colorado's fourteeners are wildly popular, climbed by people from all over the world. Thousands of people have climbed all 54 peaks. Many die-hard hikers have climbed each of them several times.

Many of our customers were climbers seeking maps of these peaks in preparation for their climbs. And many of them, while exceedingly enthusiastic, were also utterly inexperienced in the ways of the mountains. These were the ones who made me nervous.

Climbers must always expect treacherous terrain and need to be equipped with adequate food, water, clothing, and, of course, a good map and compass. Many of our customers—particularly tourists from out of state—were unprepared for the weather extremes common in the high mountains such as torrential afternoon thunderstorms, dramatic drops in temperatures, and unexpected snow even in the heat of summer.

I've climbed 38 of the fourteeners myself. I experienced snow on Yale peak, thunderstorms on Mount Huron and Longs Peak, and steep, slippery, boulder choked slopes on many others.

On a climb of Mount Elbert in late August a few years ago, my wife and I encountered a woman and her two teenage daughters. They had one bottle of water between them, were wearing shorts and sweatshirts, and had no extra food to fuel them on their climb.

My wife and I gained the summit where we were greeted by angry, black storm clouds which were hidden by the mountain as we climbed. We hastened down off the peak to avoid potential lightning strikes, and on our way down, saw the woman with one of her daughters still heading toward the summit. The storm was over the mountain by this time and we could hear the thunder and see the lightening. Then it started to snow.

We advised the woman to descend, but she didn't want to because the summit seemed so near.

"Can't give up now, we've come all this way and we're almost to the top."

She told us her other daughter was lying about one quarter mile down the trail, too tired to continue.

Still the mother refused to turn back. Her daughter, however, wanted to go back. So my wife, the daughter, and I hurried down the mountain to the other daughter, still lying beside the trail and now covered with snow. We helped her up, brushed off the snow, gave her a stocking cap and mittens to warm up, and took both girls down the mountain into the shelter of some trees to wait for their mother.

The two girls were beginning to warm up by the time their mother came down the mountain, having finally realized it was too dangerous to summit. She was cold and wet and surprised to see the extra clothes we had given to her daughters to keep them warm and dry in the rain and snow storm.

This clueless woman had no idea how lucky she and her daughters were. The top of a fourteener is no place to be when a summer storm swoops in, temperatures plummet, and lightning starts flashing.

Unfortunately, there are many people on the mountain equally unprepared. Hikers heading into the mountains without much experience and aiming to summit a fourteener, should know that mountains make their own weather. It is often unpredictable, even in the middle of summer. The oxygen at the top is much lower than what we are used to, which can sometimes cause difficulty.

Thankfully, Colorado weather is usually sunny and pleasant, and summer storms often don't roll in until afternoon. People from all over Colorado as well as the rest of the country climb the state's famous fourteeners without incident.

My advice was always simple: be prepared and enjoy yourself.

Happy hiking!

Climbing Blanca, Little Bear, and Ellingwood

One afternoon three men came into the map store wanting maps of Blanca, Little Bear, and Ellingwood Peaks, three fourteeners relatively close together on the same curving ridge. They were all in the military, strapping young men who appeared strong and fit.

The trio planned to climb to the saddle between Blanca and Ellingwood, turn north to "tap" the Ellingwood summit, then return to the saddle to spend the night. They then planned to follow the ridge south to climb Little Bear. After summiting Little Bear they intended to drop down the nearly-vertical north ridge to the valley below.

They were enthusiastic about their coming adventure but it was obvious to me that they had no idea what they were in for.

I had climbed Blanca Peak and knew it to be a difficult mountain with a long steep boulder-strewn slope to the summit. Many people do follow the Blanca ridge north and summit Ellingwood Peak after Blanca. It is about a mile distant across a boulder field all the way.

But I had seen the traverse to the Little Bear climb. Their plan seemed impossible for most climbers to accomplish in one day. I felt obliged to say something.

"How many fourteeners have you climbed?" I asked.

"We've climbed several fourteeners with no problems," said one of the three.

"Do you plan to use ropes and other climbing protection?"

"We were told ropes were not needed for this climb," another replied.

While I knew they didn't need ropes for Blanca and Ellingwood, I was pretty sure they *would* need them for Little Bear.

Another customer overheard our conversation and joined us. He asked my soldiers what experience they had in climbing a near vertical mountain face.

My unease increased when they admitted that none of them had any experience.

"Here's what you can expect," our newcomer said. "It will take you close to a full day to climb Blanca and make it back to the saddle after summiting Ellingwood. And that is only if you are strong, fast hikers.

"On the leg from the saddle to Little Bear there are a series of gendarmes (steep, pointy, rock pinnacles) so rugged, they usually prevent a traverse to Little Bear.

"You'd be better off descending Ellingwood, spending the night in the valley then ascending directly up the steep north face to the summit of Little Bear. It's difficult, but in line with the spirit of your adventure.

"You will have to ascend the 'bowling alley,' a narrow steep ravine near the summit. It's loaded with loose rocks that tend to dislodge and roll down on unsuspecting climbers below you. Climbing helmets are a must. Climbing these three peaks will take you *two full days*—if you are strong, fast, and experienced."

I was glad to hear feedback from someone more familiar with these three mountains than me. I didn't want my soldiers to get into trouble on the mountain.

The three men were a bit subdued after hearing the other climber's advice. They wisely decided to alter their plans, giving themselves more time for their grand adventure.

I was relieved that we had saved these men from a potentially tragic fate in the "bowling alley."

UTM Training

Many hikers and hunters have GPS devices, but a surprising number don't know how to use them.

The GPS units are usually set up at the factory to show latitude and longitude when setting a waypoint, a point on a map. But finding the latitude and longitude on a map is not easy.

When customers expressed difficulty using their GPS unit, I would offer them a short tutorial on how to use it. No one ever turned down my offer.

The first question I asked is if they were familiar with the UTM grid. The answer was invariably no, so that was where I began.

UTM is the acronym for Universal Transverse Mercator and is one method to project the earth—a sphere—on a flat piece of paper. The UTM system divides the earth's surface north to south into sixty zones each six degrees wide. The system is widely used in the military and is on all USGS 7 ½ minute maps.

I would show my customers two 7 ½ minute maps, one drawn with the latitude and longitude grid and one drawn with the UTM grid. The UTM grid had many more lines than the latitude longitude grid. This made it simpler to find a point on the map with the UTM grid.

The UTM grid has one kilometer squares. I never mentioned this initially because most people think they need to convert the kilometer to miles or feet, which they don't know how to do.

So I simply started with a square kilometer and broke it down into tenths to find a spot on the map that corresponded to a waypoint on their GPS unit.

When customers saw how easy this was, they became more confident using their GPS unit.

Then I showed them how to change the factory settings from latitude/longitude to UTM and how to make sure they set their GPS device to the map they were using.

I must have conducted this on-the-spot mini class hundreds of times. I always found it gratifying to help so many people become more proficient in using their GPS units. Who knows how many I saved from getting lost.

A few years ago, a national magazine published an article on how to read UTM coordinates. When I saw they had made a mistake in identifying the coordinates on a map, I emailed the editor. He replied that I was correct and they had indeed made a mistake in the article.

But as far as I know, and unfortunately for his readers, he never published the correction.

All USGS maps, Trails Illustrated maps, and most hiking maps include UTM coordinates in addition to latitude/longitude.

BLM maps on the other hand, show land ownership and latitude/longitude, but not UTM coordinates.

One customer told me he was furious with the BLM for not including UTM coordinates. He told me he had gone to the BLM office to find out who was responsible for creating their maps. It took some persistent questioning but he finally was able to find the one man responsible for removing the UTM grid.

When asked why he removed the grid, the mapmaker replied simply, "I don't think we need it."

I can just imagine the earful he got from my angry customer. People depend on maps, and I learned over the years that they take them very seriously. Perhaps too seriously in this case.

Or perhaps not. Using a GPS unit and a map with a UTM grid is an excellent way to pinpoint your location and keep from getting lost. I speak from experience. I once lost my way traveling through the La Garita Wilderness en route to the Wheeler Geologic area.

But a quick check of my UTM device pinpointed where I was on my map and I soon was back on track.

From Finding Maps
to Tying Ties

Working at the map store required me to be a man of many talents.

Although nearly all of the USGS Map Store customers come to buy maps, occasionally someone came in for an entirely different reason.

One day a distressed-looking mother and her teenage son rushed in. The young man was dressed in a suit and dress shirt, but his mother was holding his necktie.

"Can you tie a necktie?" she asked me.

"Of course. What do you need?"

"My son has an interview here in a few minutes for a job as an intern and he doesn't know how to properly tie a knot in his tie. Can you help him with that?"

I'd worn a tie for more than 30 years during my marketing career so I'd had lots of practice.

The mother handed me the tie. "We tried to tie it but it never came out right," she said. "We looked on the Internet and tried to follow the instructions but they didn't work."

As I assisted with the tie, the young man was obviously nervous, so I asked him to tell me about the internship he was applying for.

"It's a full-time summer job assisting one of the USGS scientists conducting environmental research. I'm going up against twenty other applicants."

By now I was tightening the knot against his collar. "Will this internship include fieldwork?"

"I don't know. I'll find out more details of what I'll be doing during the interview."

I handed him a small mirror to check out his tie, and he seemed very pleased, nodding and glancing at his mother. (I was pleased to find my necktie tying skills were still intact.)

"Good luck in your interview, and be sure to stop by and let me know how it went."

"You can count on it, and thanks for helping me with the tie."

He never came back to the store and I never learned if he got the job.

But I hoped his neat and professional-looking tie helped him make a good impression in his interview.

Wideawake

I thought I knew the area around Central City quite well, but when a young, bearded customer asked for a map of the town of Wideawake one day, I was stumped.

My customer told me Wideawake was north of Central City and east of Apex. I knew that Apex was on the Central City map, so I pulled it from the shelf and placed it on the table in front of him.

Turns out, Wideawake is a deserted ghost town reached only by an unmarked four-wheel-drive road. It's seven miles from the nearest town. Little remains of Wideawake today, except for an old cabin and a few foundations. The last known resident, a retired shepherd, died in 1964.

My customer looked carefully at the map for a while then looked up at me, smiled, and began an extraordinary tale.

"You see this road junction here?" he asked. "I was there a few weeks ago doing a bit of exploring and looking for interesting artifacts. There is a cabin just east of this junction.

"I'm a diviner," he continued, "and I can find almost anything buried by using my divining rods. In the old days, people often buried things beneath the floorboards and then left or died, and the buried items were never recovered. So I started divining in this cabin, and I came upon the remains of a buried man.

"I can tell the difference between a man and a woman in a grave because of the different signatures I get from the divining rods."

I was a bit skeptical but listened as he continued his story.

"I kept divining in the cabin and found two more graves, a man and a woman. When I didn't find anything more, I went outside and started divining around the cabin. And lo and behold, I found five more graves.

By now I was starting to get a bad feeling because you don't often find so many graves in the same area unless it's a cemetery. I was concerned about what happened there, so I decided to go to the county sheriff and tell him what I had found.

"The sheriff didn't believe my story and he especially didn't believe I could determine if a grave held a man or a woman using my divining rods.

"To prove I was telling the truth, I convinced him to come with me to the local cemetery and stand in front of a headstone so I couldn't see the name on it. I would divine the grave and tell him if the grave was that of a man or a woman.

"We went out to the cemetery and I divined the graves. I was right five out of five times!"

His story was getting more interesting.

"After the demonstration at the cemetery, the sheriff agreed to come with me to the abandoned cabin. I divined in the cabin and around the area outside, showing the sheriff the location of all the graves.

"After he saw all the graves I found, he asked me if I thought a crime had been committed there. I told him I had no idea. That was his department. But I wasn't about to go digging up any graves to see what was buried. He agreed and told me it was against the law to dig up graves.

"The sheriff then told me to leave and never come back to the area ever again!"

My eyes widened at that.

"Can he do that?" the customer asked me, amazed by the sheriff's order. "This is national forest land."

I wasn't sure, but I doubted the sheriff had the authority to ban him from public lands. Bob, an employee of the Forest Service which shared space in the map store, came over and agreed that the sheriff had no authority to keep him off national forest land.

"I haven't been back since the sheriff told me to keep away. I don't want any trouble," he told me.

I thought he had finished his story, but it suddenly got even more bizarre.

"A few days after my run-in with the sheriff," he continued, "I was having coffee at a coffee shop in Nederland. A woman to my left was reading the palm of a guy next to her.

"When she finished reading his palm, she turned to me. I've never believed in that palm reading stuff, so I kept my hands at my side because I didn't want her reading my palm, even by accident.

"But then she said 'And you, you better stop looking for dead people or you will be dead yourself within two years!'

"She scared the devil out of me with that and I haven't been back to the cabin since!"

"Had you ever met this woman before?" I asked.

"Never seen her before in my life."

"Do you still want to go back to the cabin and do some more divining?"

"No way!" he said.

"There are lots of other places to go divining without divining for dead people."

After he left with his map of Wideawake, I wondered what other mysteries he might find divining around other old ghost towns. The Rockies are loaded with them, over 600, perhaps just waiting for people like him to come along so they can finally give up their long-buried secrets.

Hole in the Arctic to the Center of the Earth

The Antarctic is mapped in detail, showing the topography of the mountains, the South Pole, and even the dry valleys where high winds scour the snow down to bare, frozen earth.

But no maps exist of the Arctic.

And my customer was quite disappointed.

"You see," he said with authority, "I want a map of the Arctic to see if your maps show the giant hole that leads to the center of the earth."

I did my best to hide my amusement.

He handed me a booklet. "Here. This explains the whole thing."

The booklet explained the "hollow earth theory" and included at least a dozen pictures showing a hole in the arctic sea ice...one that supposedly led to the center of the earth. It had been printed from an Internet website and placed in a three ring folder.

"The pictures are from NASA, taken by satellite," he explained. "I know they are real because I found them on the Internet. I made copies of the pictures and included them in this booklet as proof of the hole to the hollow earth."

Now, first of all, the idea that someone would believe something is real just because they found it on the Internet dumbfounded me. But I wasn't inclined to argue. Instead, I looked at the aerial photos showing a mass of clouds with a circular break in them. But nothing was visible below the break.

"The earth is completely hollow," my odd customer went on, "and has a race of very tall people living in it. They are tall because gravity is almost nonexistent in there. So gravity does not hold them down as they grow.

"They are also more spiritually and intellectually advanced than we are and are connected with the third, fourth, and fifth dimensions in ways that we are not. We suspect that they descended from the ancient Mayan culture which mysteriously disappeared hundreds of years ago, but no one knows for sure."

I might have nodded. I might have gaped. I might have laughed, but only inwardly to myself.

"There is an atomic sun in the center and daylight 24 hours a day. There are also several continents in the hollow earth, all separated by freshwater oceans," he went on.

"Has anyone been to the hollow earth and returned?" I asked.

"Absolutely!" he replied. "Admiral Byrd found a deep crack in the Antarctic ice when he was searching for the South Pole. He followed the crack and ended up in the hollow earth. He wrote about it in his journal. You can read all about it on the Internet."

"Have you been there?" I asked.

"Not yet," he said, "but I'm saving up so I will have enough money to travel to Siberia, get on a Russian icebreaker, and get near the hole. No ships go all the way to the hole, so I will need to walk the last few miles myself."

"Walk miles across the Arctic ice? But won't you fall into the hole when you get there?" I asked.

"Yes, that's the whole idea. You see, the gravitational field is halfway between the inner and the outer crusts of the earth," he answered. "I will fall with the force of gravity until I get halfway down into the hole. Gravity will then repel me for the last half. After that I will slow down until I reach the world inside and can walk out of the hole.

"Then I will be inside the earth and can explore it as long as I like. I may even decide to stay there."

It was one of the most bizarre theories I had ever heard, but my customer was completely convinced of it. I realized that any attempts to point out geological facts to the contrary would be fruitless.

As he left, I wished him good luck on his journey to the center of the earth.

"Be sure to come back after your visit to tell me what you saw," I told him.

"Thank you," he said. "I certainly will. And you can keep this copy of my booklet. I have more."

He walked out of the store in cheerful anticipation of his grand and wonderful adventure.

Curious, I did a web search of the *hollow earth theory* after he left. To my surprise, I found dozens of websites on the subject.

But I never saw my customer again.

Perhaps he is still in the center of the earth.

Water Witcher

One customer at the map store was a frequent visitor and knew where to look for the maps that interested him without any help from me. In his fifties, was stocky and always impeccably dressed.

On each visit he did the same thing—after looking at a map index he would retrieve a 7 ½ minute map from the map shelves, place it on a table, and examine it in detail.

Then he'd pull a small brass device from his pocket and hold it over the map. It was pointed on one end, about one inch in diameter and looked just like a plumb bob. The customer would hold it above the map by a string, then slowly move the plumb bob over the map.

After seeing this several times, I finally asked him what he was doing.

"I'm witching for water," was the strange reply.

Water witching has always been a mystery to me. I'd seen water witching before, but only outdoors by someone holding a forked water-witching stick.

I am of two minds concerning water witchers— also known as diviners or dowsers—people who use divining rods to find water. On the one hand they seem like charlatans, pretending that their diving rods move by themselves. On the other hand, I've seen them work with my own eyes.

They do find water. I once drilled for water on land I owned and the drilling operator successfully used a forked branch as a witching stick to find the right drill site.

Even so, for me the jury is still out—I could go either way.

"How can you find water using only a map?" I asked.

"I don't have a scientific explanation," he answered. "All I know is that it works."

He held the device over the map slowly moving it back and forth. Suddenly his hand, arm, and shoulder began to shake and tremble and the device began to swing wildly back and forth.

He had found water. Or so he claimed.

I was skeptical. "Seems to me that the device is moving because you are moving your arm."

"I have no control over my hand and arm when I find water," he said. "They move of their own accord. I don't move them. My arm is what tells me where the water is and the witching device tells me even more precisely. Once I use the map to find water, I go to that location in person and verify on the ground where to drill."

Although I had seen a witching fork work in my own case, using a plumb bob on a map was new to me. But my customer said he had been witching this way for years and swore by it.

Whatever works.

Bakken

Geologists have known of the existence of shale oil in the Bakken shale formation in North Dakota for decades.

But the Bakken formation is a relatively thin layer of shale and traditional drilling techniques are neither efficient nor cost effective.

Horizontal drilling techniques have recently made oil in the Bakken formation more readily available and obtaining it cost effective. Ground zero for drilling in the Bakken oil field is the Williston area of North Dakota. That fine state is reaping the benefits. At the time of this writing, state unemployment was down around three per cent and the state government boasted a sizeable budget surplus — a rarity among states or any government.

The irresistible lure of high-paying jobs and easy money brought about a corresponding interest in maps of the area. So when a young man entered the store asking for maps around the Williston area, I was not surprised.

"Are you looking to get a piece of the Bakken field?" I asked as I began searching for his maps.

His was obviously taken aback. "How did you know?"

It was as though he knew a secret and was surprised as well as disappointed that I so quickly guessed it.

"You aren't the first person to come in here asking about the Bakken field. The oil activity up there isn't exactly a secret, and a number of geologists have come to the map store to get maps of the same area," I replied. "They speak freely about the Bakken field and generally keep us up to date on drilling activities."

This customer was not a geologist. He wanted to determine which lands were private and which were public and how to buy public land, usually BLM land. It seemed my customer was looking for a get-rich-quick scheme. And he was hardly the first.

I directed him to the BLM office. "Ask the BLM if they have any land in the area they plan to lease. You could put in a bid, with the hope of buying oil and mineral rights near the Bakken field and selling the rights to oil companies for a profit. But I have to tell you, I suspect much, if not all, of this valuable land had been purchased long ago by oil companies."

My customer was not deterred by my cautions. He headed for the checkout counter with his North Dakota maps of the Williston area. I could tell that to him, they were as good as treasure maps. As good as gold.

I sincerely wished him luck as he left the store in search of his own personal version of the American dream.

Lady Silverheels

There are many colorful legends in Colorado's history, but the legend of Lady Silverheels is one of my favorites.

Silverheels was a mysterious figure about whom very little is known—a simple dance-hall girl who heroically sacrificed herself to save a small mining community from a devastating plague.

As the legend goes, in the mid 1800s, a beautiful young woman with lush dark hair and a long black dress stepped out of the Denver stage coach at Buckskin Joe. At that time, Buckskin Joe was a bustling mining community at the base of a mountain near Alma, with a population of 5,000 eager-to-get-rich souls.

Before long, the comely young woman landed a job as a dance hall girl at Bill Buck's dance hall. Her trademark feature, a pair of shoes with the heels clad in pure silver, gave her the name Lady Silverheels.

As Buck's newest "fancy lady," Lady Silverheels was an instant hit. She smiled, sang, and danced her way into the hearts of the roughest of miners. Multiple men proposed marriage.

Lady Silverheels pulled in gold for Bill Buck's dance hall. She became a regular dancer and her reputation spread as miners from other nearby mining towns traveled to Buckskin Joe. At Bill Buck's, they spent the precious gold they mined for a chance to dance with Lady Silverheels.

Then, in the fall of 1861, two miners came into town carrying a disease that would nearly destroy the town.

The miners had traveled from the San Luis valley and stopped at Buckskin Joe to rest. Shortly after arriving, one of the miners became mysteriously ill and died by the end of the day. His companion soon also fell ill and died.

Smallpox had arrived at Buckskin Joe.

The disease started with flu symptoms but soon became much worse, claiming the lives of most of those who fell ill. Denver, Colorado Springs, and Leadville were telegraphed for doctors and nurses to help. But few, if any, would risk their lives working to halt the spread of this deadly disease. The town's own residents fled as word of the plague spread. Businesses closed and Buckskin Joe became a ghost town.

In the midst of this tragedy the legend of Lady Silverheels was born.

With little regard for her own health and safety, Lady Silverheels stayed at Buckskin Joe, caring for the diseased and dying men in the mining camp. Every day she walked in the cold from cabin to cabin, visiting the sick miners, administering medicine, and providing food and care to the ailing men.

Eventually the plague ran its course and the town's residents slowly returned.

But in the final days of the epidemic Lady Silverheels became infected. She secluded herself in her small cabin and suffered in silence, cared for only by an elderly resident called Aunt Martha.

The town healed and slowly returned to normal, but Lady Silverheels remained secluded. The townsfolk talked of nothing else, wondering if her beauty had been badly marred, if she would ever dance again.

One evening Lady Silverheels asked Aunt Martha to help her dress and tie up her hair. She then bid Aunt Martha goodnight.

Meanwhile, the miners at Buckskin Joe, impatient to see their nurturing Lady Silverheels, had taken up a collection to give her as a show of gratitude. But when they took their gift to her cabin, it was empty.

Lady Silverheels had disappeared.

A search began immediately. Aunt Martha was as confused as everyone else as to the whereabouts of Lady Silverheels. The miners found nothing in their search and many feared the worst.

Some speculated that rather than face her admirers with her face scarred by smallpox, she had simply walked into the mountains and died. She was never seen again.

Lady Silverheel's fate may never be known. The miners named the mountain north of Buckskin Joe in her honor — Mount Silverheels.

But the legend does not end here. Some say that after the plague, people saw an unknown woman dressed in black walking among the graves of the miners who died during those terrible days. Others say Lady Silverheels still walks the flanks of her namesake mountain to this day.

Knowing this legend, I was immediately intrigued when a customer entered the store and asked for a map of Mount Silverheels.

"Do you know the legend of Silverheels?" I asked.

His eyes twinkled as he told me his story.

"I was on a hike to the summit of the mountain earlier this year," he began. "The trail was not well marked and I lost it in the forest at the base of the peak. When I retraced my steps to determine where I had gone wrong, I ran into a woman as she emerged from a small trail in the forest. She wore a sun hat and dark glasses, and had long thick dark hair. Her hat was angled in such a way as to cast a shadow over her face, and I wasn't able to guess her age.

"I told her I was looking for the trail to the summit of Silverheels and asked her if she knew it and could help me find it. She directed me back down the trail I had come up to a small mining cabin I'd just passed, told me to turn directly west at the cabin and I would find the summit trail.

"To be friendly, I asked if she hiked here often. A smile I can only describe as knowing flitted across her face. She said she had lived nearby for a long time and frequently hiked these woods. As I turned to go back down the trail to the cabin I realized I hadn't thanked her.

"But when I turned around, she had vanished. The trees were not that thick and I should have been able to see her walking away for quite a distance. I've never understood how she could have disappeared so quietly and so quickly.

"Then I recalled the legend. Was my guide who appeared and disappeared so suddenly the ghost of Lady Silverheels? Of course not, it's just a legend, I told myself. She must have been a local, probably out for a morning walk."

A small shiver crept down my spine at the end of his tale. We looked at each other, neither one of us quite ready to agree that he had seen the ghost of the legendary Lady Silverheels.

After all, there could have been some other perfectly logical explanation. Right?

Mapsco

The USGS was the single source for its 7 ½ minute topographical maps. It sold them to thousands of map stores across the country. One of these was Mapsco, a well known map store on South Broadway Street in Denver.

Mapsco not only sold all the Colorado USGS topographical maps, but a wide variety of Trails Illustrated maps, globes, road atlases, books, trail guides, antique maps, and other items as well. It was also a popular source in the Denver area for international maps.

Mapsco was launched in 1952 with the publication of a street atlas of Dallas, Texas. Sales gradually grew and in 1971 the company introduced its second product, a street atlas of Fort Worth. By the late 1990s, Mapsco had nine sales outlets in Texas, Colorado, and other western states. But over the years, sales gradually began to fall and the Denver store closed in April 2010.

Like USGS map store customers, many Mapsco customers had interesting and unusual stories to tell about the maps they came in to buy.

The following stories are from the Mapsco map store and were contributed by Roland Holtz, the last manager of Mapsco and later, manager of the USGS map store.

Lamination Disaster

Old maps hold a special fascination for those of us who work in a map store. So when a white-haired man strolled into the Mapsco store with his wife and said he had an old map he wanted to preserve, the staff was immediately interested.

"What do you have?" Roland asked.

Slowly and lovingly the man unrolled his map. "This is a map of the Gila National Forest printed in 1931. I received it from the University of New Mexico many years ago as a retirement gift. I was a professor of geology at the university for over 30 years and conducted much of my research in the Gila National Forest. I kept the map in my closet these past years, but now I would like to laminate it and preserve it so I can display it in my home. Can you help me?"

Mapsco was one of the few places that had the facilities to laminate large maps. The map was beautiful, in perfect condition, and a rare find. Roland was eager to tackle the job.

But laminating large maps was not without risk.

"Yes, we can laminate this map," Roland told his customer. "But I need to tell you that we occasionally have problems with maps this large. About one in ten large maps don't laminate well, but this map is in excellent condition with no folds or tears. It should laminate without problems. Do you want us to go ahead?"

"Yes," the man replied. "I'll take my chances."

Laminating is a simple concept but difficult to execute. The laminating machine consists of two large rolls of laminate material—a thin plastic—one above the other. The map to be laminated is carefully placed between these two rolls. Slowly the machine pulls the map through the rolls which sandwich the map between the laminate. This sandwich of map and laminate is then drawn through a set of heated rollers that fuse the laminate to the map and produce a laminated product.

The plastic and the map must be smooth and completely without wrinkles.

In this case, the staff took extra care in positioning the laminate material and the map in the laminating machine. When all was ready, the staff pressed the start button and the map crawled through the rollers.

At first the map and laminating sandwich went through the machine perfectly.

But about halfway through the machine, the map twisted ever so slightly. Everyone held their breath hoping it would straighten out. But the map began to wrinkle, at first just a little, then more and more.

Everyone stared in disbelief as the map wrinkled and twisted in slow motion into ruin before their eyes. The map was beyond repair. The laminate material was fused to the paper and was impossible to remove.

The entire Mapsco staff was in a state of near panic. They tried to figure out what they could do.

The only answer seemed to be to try to replace the map.

But first they needed to tell their customer what just happened to his beloved map.

"We had problems in the laminating process," Roland told him. "The laminating machine malfunctioned, wrinkled the map, and it is beyond repair. We are so sorry this happened."

Their customer remained surprisingly calm, and his response was understated but to the point.

"What do you intend to do?"

"We plan to contact every map store we can until we find another map like this and replace your damaged map," Roland replied. "It may take some time, but we will leave no stone unturned until we make this right."

The customer thanked Roland for his efforts and said he would expect to hear from him. But he was visibly disappointed and it was apparent he doubted the search would be successful.

The search for a replacement map began immediately with a call to the U S. Forest Service. No luck. The staff asked for a check of the Forest Service archives. Nothing. They called one map store after another, first in New Mexico, then other western states. Still nothing.

They tried other map stores across the country. All to no avail. No one had a 1931 map of the Gila National Forest.

Then someone had the bright idea to contact the Library of Congress. Supposedly they had a copy of everything published with a Library of Congress number. The damaged 1931 map of the Gila National Forest had a number the staff could read. Finally, a glimmer of hope.

A call to the Library of Congress determined it did indeed have a copy of the map. It was an electronic copy, but a copy that could be printed if they wanted. Of course the staff wanted a printed copy. So the necessary arrangements were made and they waited for it to arrive.

Greatly relieved, Roland phoned his customer to tell him the good news.

A few weeks later the map arrived and the staff carefully opened the package. To their dismay, the map was blurry and almost impossible to read.

They called the Library of Congress for an explanation but were told their printer had simply printed what was on file. The staff asked for a copy of the file and received an electronic copy later that day.

Upon receipt of the file, the staff asked Mapsco's internal computer expert to review it. After closely examining it she said it was corrupted and that she could not print a clean copy. Could she fix it? She didn't know. But she would try.

The expert went to work attempting to align the images to produce a clean file. Her work took several days and she appeared hopeful. Everyone was encouraged. Finally she gave the good news the staff had hoped and prayed for.

The file was now in good shape.

A copy was printed and the map emerged clear and sharp. Everyone was delighted and thrilled. Now if they could laminate it, their problem would be solved.

Carefully the staff placed the map between the laminate material, positioned the sandwich in the laminate machine and pressed the start button.

No one moved.

Slowly the map emerged from the machine — this time with no wrinkles.

The staff breathed a collective sigh of relief and Roland called the map owner.

The next day a very pleased white-haired man came into the store to pick up his newly laminated 1931 Gila National Forest map.

The Shaman

One afternoon the mellow sounds of a pan flute came drifting through the Mapsco store.

Heads turned to the figure who had just walked in. He was dressed head to toe in buckskin. He wore his long, black hair tied back in a ponytail, had moccasins on his feet, and carried a tambourine and a pan flute. Around his neck were several colorful bead necklaces. He was smiling broadly.

Roland asked if he could be of help.

"I just received my official certification as an Indian Shaman," the man in buckskin announced proudly. "I am here to bring peace to the world. I plan to travel to the corners of the earth where the four winds blow and I will bless our Mother the Earth at each of the four winds."

Roland thought of asking him exactly how he would explain that there are "corners of the earth" when the earth is a sphere and therefore doesn't have corners. And how would he explain that wind doesn't start from a specific point, but rather follows the high and low pressure systems that account for global surface winds.

But somehow Roland felt his questions would be in vain, so he just played along. "What exactly do you need?"

"I need a map showing where the four winds blow and I have the latitude and longitude coordinates to help you find these places on the earth," he replied.

He gave Roland the coordinates, and Roland told him he would look on a map program to find the coordinates.

As he began his search, the Shaman played his pan flute. He was getting a lot of interest, as well as some nervous looks from the other customers in the store, but he didn't seem to mind.

"Where did you get the coordinates?" Roland asked.

"I conjured them up during my shaman training. I went into a trance thinking about the four winds and the coordinates just popped into my head," the newly minted shaman said helpfully.

Roland continued to look for the coordinates on his world map program and after a while, he did find their locations. One was in the South Pacific, another in the Atlantic, one in the Arctic, and the last in the very center of Russia.

Roland printed out a map showing the coordinate locations and gave it the shaman. "What do you plan to do now that you know where the coordinates are?"

"My wife and I are going on a life-long journey," the shaman replied. "This is my destiny. We will travel to the four points on the map, find where the four winds begin to blow and bless the earth with my new shaman powers. I believe this will begin to heal the earth and bring a lasting peace for all mankind."

He paid for his map and Roland wished him luck on his journey.

Heads turned to the mellow sounds of his pan flute that followed him out the door.

Whether or not he would bring peace to the earth, the shaman had certainly brought a peaceful feeling to Mapsco. And much merriment as the customers and staff discussed the shaman and his quest.

Visit Us Online

Visit the Bristlecone Publishing books
at the following websites:

www.TopoTheBook.com

www.WheresMyFootball.com

At these websites you will find:
Author information
Book excerpts
Book summaries
And much more

BRISTLECONE
PUBLISHING

Bristlecone Publishing
Lakewood, Colorado

Made in the USA
Middletown, DE
19 October 2022